Coffeehouse SONGS

PREFACE

Learning to play a musical instrument is one of the most satisfying experiences a person can have. Being able to play along with other musicians makes that even more rewarding. This collection of coffeehouse songs is designed to make it easy to enjoy the fun of gathering with friends and family to make music together.

The selections in this book include a wide variety of songs drawn from several generations of popular music. These songs will provide fun opportunities to make music with other players. The music for each song displays the chord diagrams for five instruments: ukulele, baritone ukulele, guitar, mandolin and banjo. The chord diagrams indicate basic, commonly used finger positions. More advanced players can substitute alternate chord formations.

It is easy to find recordings of all these tunes performed by outstanding musicians. Listening can help you understand more about the style as you and your friends play these songs.

Arranged by Mark Phillips

ISBN 978-1-7051-1306-6

Visit Hal Leonard Online at
www.halleonard.com

Contact us:
Hal Leonard
7777 West Bluemound Road
Milwaukee, WI 53213
Email: info@halleonard.com

In Europe, contact:
Hal Leonard Europe Limited
42 Wigmore Street
Marylebone, London, W1U 2RN
Email: info@halleonardeurope.com

In Australia, contact:
Hal Leonard Aust
4 Lentara Court
Cheltenham, Victor
Email: info@halleo

Standard Ukulele

C	Cmaj7	Em	Dm7	G7	Fm	F
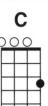	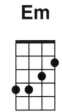	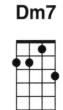	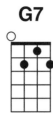	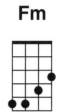	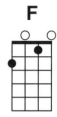	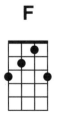

Baritone Ukulele

C	Cmaj7	Em	Dm7	G7	Fm	F
	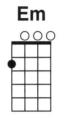	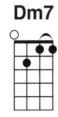	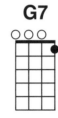			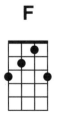

Guitar

C	Cmaj7	Em	Dm7	G7	Fm	F
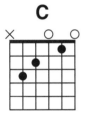	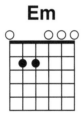	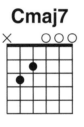	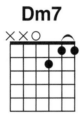	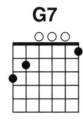		

Mandolin

C	Cmaj7	Em	Dm7	G7	Fm	F
	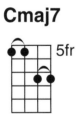 5fr	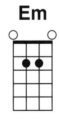	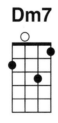			

Banjo

C	Cmaj7	Em	Dm7	G7	Fm	F
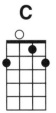	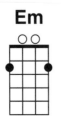	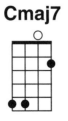	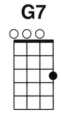	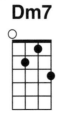		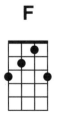

Across the Universe

Words and Music by John Lennon and Paul McCartney

Verse
Slow

1. Words are flow-ing out like end-less rain in-to a pa-per cup. They
Pools of sor-row, waves of joy are drift-ing through my o-pened mind, pos-

slith-er while they pass, they slip a - way a-cross the u-ni-verse.
sess-ing and ca-

𝄋 Chorus

ress-ing me. __ Jai __ Gu-ru __ De - va. __ Om.

Noth-ing's gon-na change my world, __ noth-ing's gon-na change my world. __

2nd time, to Coda ⊕ Verse
3rd time, Fine

2. Im-ag-es of bro-ken light which dance be-fore me like a mil-lion
Thoughts me-an-der like a rest-less wind in-side a let-ter box. They

D.S. al Coda
(take repeat)

eyes, they call me on and on a-cross the u-ni-verse.
tum-ble blind-ly as they make their way a-cross the u-ni-verse.

⊕ Coda/Verse

3. Sounds of laugh-ter, shades of earth are ring-ing through my o-pened ears, in -
Lim-it-less un-dy-ing love which shines a-round me like a mil-lion

D.S. al Fine
(take repeat)

cit-ing and in - vit-ing me. __ suns, and calls me on and on a-cross the u-ni-verse.

Standard Ukulele

F	C	Em	Am	G	B♭	Gsus4	E7
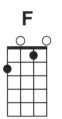	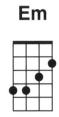	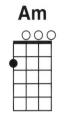			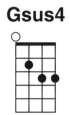	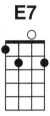	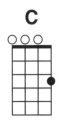

Baritone Ukulele

F	C	Em	Am	G	B♭	Gsus4	E7
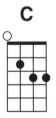				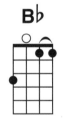	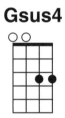		

Guitar

F	C	Em	Am	G	B♭	Gsus4	E7
	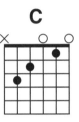		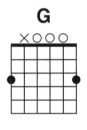	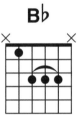		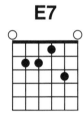	

Mandolin

F	C	Em	Am	G	B♭	Gsus4	E7
	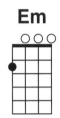				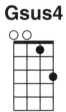	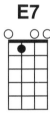	

Banjo

F	C	Em	Am	G	B♭	Gsus4	E7
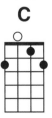	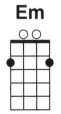	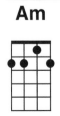	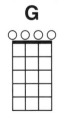	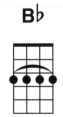	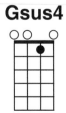	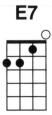	

Alison

Words and Music by Elvis Costello

Additional Lyrics

2. Well, I see you've got a husband now.
   Did he leave your pretty fingers lying in the wedding cake?
   You used to hold him right in your hand.
   I'll bet he took all he could take.
   Sometimes I wish that I could stop you from talking
   When I hear the silly things that you say.
   I think somebody better put out the big light,
   'Cause I can't stand to see you this way.

Standard Ukulele

G	C	D	Em	Bm	Am	Gsus4
	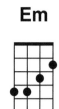	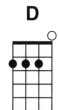	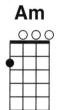			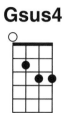

Baritone Ukulele

G	C	D	Em	Bm	Am	Gsus4
	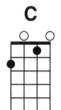	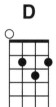	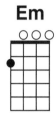	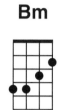	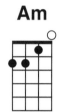	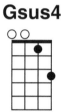

Guitar

G	C	D	Em	Bm	Am	Gsus4
	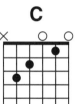	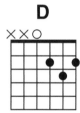	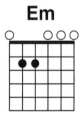			

Mandolin

G	C	D	Em	Bm	Am	Gsus4
	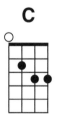	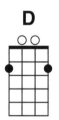	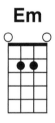	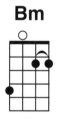	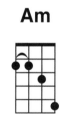	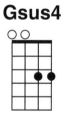

Banjo

G	C	D	Em	Bm	Am	Gsus4
	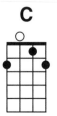	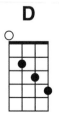	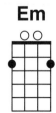	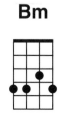	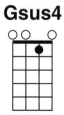	

Annie's Song

Words and Music by John Denver

*Substitute small notes 2nd & 3rd times (next 8 meas.)

Standard Ukulele

C	G	D	G5	G5(maj7)

Baritone Ukulele

C	G	D	G5	G5(maj7)

Guitar

C	G	D	G5	G5(maj7)
			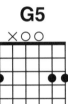	

Mandolin

C	G	D	G5	G5(maj7)
		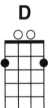		

Banjo

C	G	D	G5	G5(maj7)

Big Yellow Taxi

Words and Music by Joni Mitchell

Verse
Moderately, in 2

1. They paved par-a-dise, put up a park-ing lot ___
2., 3., 4. *See additional lyrics*

with a pink ___ ho-tel, ___ a bou-tique and a swing-

Chorus

-in' hot ___ spot. ___ Don't it al-ways seem ___ to go that you

don't know what ___ you've got ___ till it's gone? They paved par-a-dise,

put up a park-ing lot. ___
(Shoo, ___ bop, ___ bop, bop, ___ bop. Shoo, ___ bop, ___

1.
___ bop, bop, ___ bop.)
2. They

2., 3.
___ bop, bop, ___ bop.)

4.
___ bop, bop, ___ bop.)
They

paved par-a-dise, put up a park-ing lot. ___

Additional Lyrics

2. They took all the trees, put 'em in a tree museum,
   And they charged the people a dollar and a half just to see 'em.

3. Hey, farmer, farmer, put away that DDT now.
   Give me spots on my apples but leave me the birds and the bees, please.

4. Late last night I heard the screen door slam,
   And a big yellow taxi took away my old man.

Standard Ukulele

Am	F	G	C
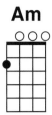	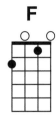	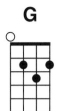	

Baritone Ukulele

Am	F	G	C
		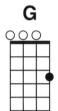	

Guitar

Am	F	G	C
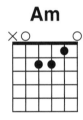	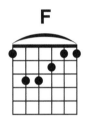	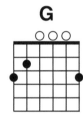	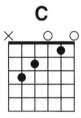

Mandolin

Am	F	G	C
	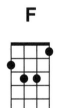	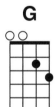	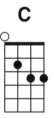

Banjo

Am	F	G	C

The Boys of Summer

Words and Music by Mike Campbell and Don Henley

Verse
Moderately, in 2

Am

1. No-bod-y on the road, __ no-bod-y on the beach. __
2., 3. *See additional lyrics*

F

I feel it in the air. The sum-mer's out of reach.

G

Emp - ty lake, __ emp - ty streets. __ The sun goes down a - lone. __

F

I'm driv - in' by your house though I know you're not home. __

Chorus

C   G

But I can see you, __ your brown skin shin - in' in the sun.

F

{ You got your hair combed back and your sun-glass - es on, ba - by.
  I see you walk-in' real slow and you're smil - in' at ev - 'ry - one. __
  You got the top pulled down and the ra - di - o on, ba - by. }

C   G

And I can tell you my love for you __ will still be strong

F   Play 3 times C

af - ter __ the boys __ of sum - mer __ have gone. __

Additional Lyrics

2. I never will forget those nights.
   I wonder if it was a dream.
   Remember how you made me crazy?
   Remember how I made you scream?
   Now I don't understand
   What happened to our love.
   But, babe, I'm gonna get you back.
   I'm gonna show you what I'm made of.

3. Out on the road today
   I saw a "Deadhead" sticker on a Cadillac.
   A little voice inside my head said,
   "Don't look back. You can never look back."
   I thought I knew what love was.
   What did I know?
   Those days are gone forever.
   I should just let 'em go, but…

Standard Ukulele

G	C	D
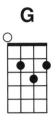	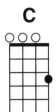	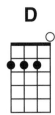

Baritone Ukulele

G	C	D
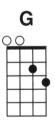	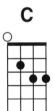	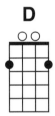

Guitar

G	C	D
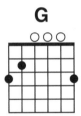	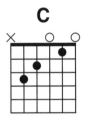	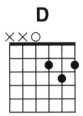

Mandolin

G	C	D
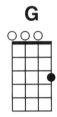	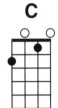	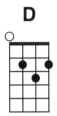

Banjo

G	C	D
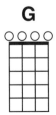	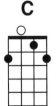	

Budapest

Words and Music by George Barnett and Joel Pott

Verse
Moderately fast

1. My house in Bu-da-pest, my, ___ my hid-den treas-ure chest, ___ gold-en grand pi-an-o, ___ my beau-ti-ful cas-til-lo. You, oo, ___ you, oo, ___ I'd leave it all.

% Verse

2. My a-cres of a land ___
3., 4., 5. *See additional lyrics*

I have a-chieved, it may be hard for you to ___ stop and be-lieve. ___ But for you, oo, ___ you, oo, ___ I'd leave it all. Oh, for you, oo, ___ you, oo, ___ I'd leave it all.

Fine

Chorus

Give me one good rea-son why I ___ should nev-er make a change. ___

Play 3 times
3rd time, D.S. al Fine

Ba-by, if you hold me, then all ___ of this will go ___ a-way. ___

Additional Lyrics

3. My many artifacts, the list goes on.
   If you just say the words, I'll, I'll up and run.
   Oh, to you, oo, you, oo, I'd leave it all.
   Oh, to you, oo, you, oo, I'd leave it all.

4. My friends and family, they don't understand.
   They fear they'll lose so much if you take my hand.
   But, for you, oo, you, oo, I'd lose it all.
   Oh, for you, oo, you, oo, I'd lose it all.

5. My house in Budapest, my, my hidden treasure chest,
   Golden grand piano, my beautiful castillo.
   You, oo, you, oo, I'd leave it all.
   Oh, for you, oo, you, oo, I'd leave it all.

Standard Ukulele

G	Em	C	D
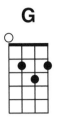	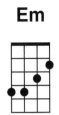	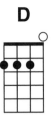	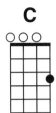

Baritone Ukulele

G	Em	C	D
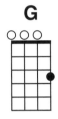	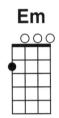	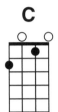	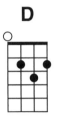

Guitar

G	Em	C	D
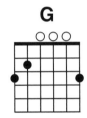	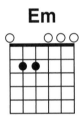	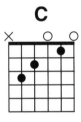	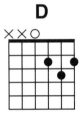

Mandolin

G	Em	C	D
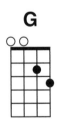	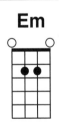	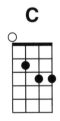	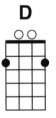

Banjo

G	Em	C	D
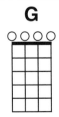	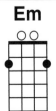	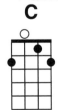	

Burn One Down

Words and Music by Ben Harper

Additional Lyrics

2. My choice is what I choose to do,
And if I'm causing no harm, it shouldn't bother you.
Your choice is who you choose to be,
And if you're causing no harm, then you're all right with me.

3. Herb, the gift from the earth,
And what's from the earth is of the greatest worth.
So before you knock it, try it first.
Oh, you'll see it's a blessing and it's not a curse.

Standard Ukulele

Gsus2 **D** **Dm** **A** **C** **E** **Bm** **C#m**

Baritone Ukulele

Gsus2 **D** **Dm** **A** **C** **E** **Bm** **C#m**

Guitar

Gsus2 **D** **Dm** **A** **C** **E** **Bm** **C#m**

 4fr

Mandolin

Gsus2 **D** **Dm** **A** **C** **E** **Bm** **C#m**

Banjo

Gsus2 **D** **Dm** **A** **C** **E** **Bm** **C#m**

Can't Find My Way Home

Words and Music by Steve Winwood

Verse
Moderately slow

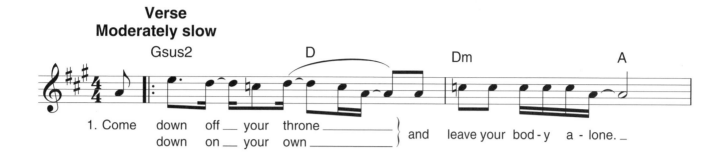

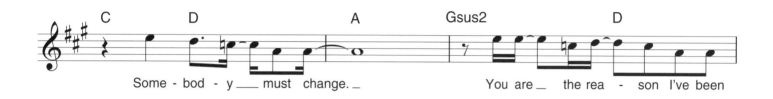

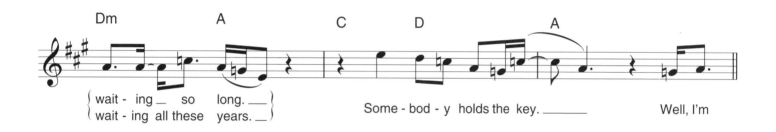

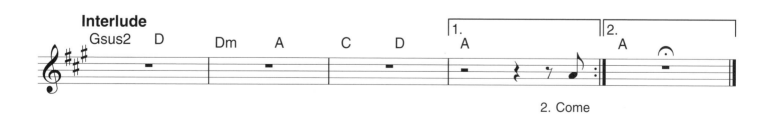

Standard Ukulele

C	F	G	G7
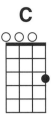	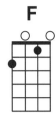		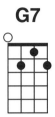

Baritone Ukulele

C	F	G	G7
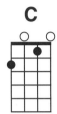		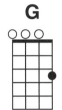	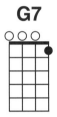

Guitar

C	F	G	G7
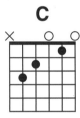	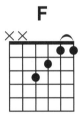	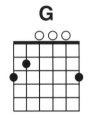	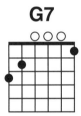

Mandolin

C	F	G	G7
	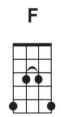	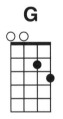	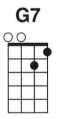

Banjo

C	F	G	G7
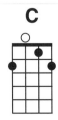		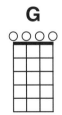	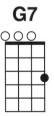

Catch the Wind

Words and Music by Donovan Leitch

Standard Ukulele

C	F	G7	Em	Dm7
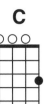	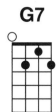		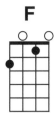	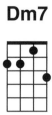

Baritone Ukulele

C	F	G7	Em	Dm7
	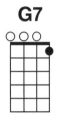	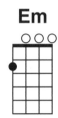		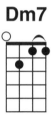

Guitar

C	F	G7	Em	Dm7
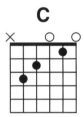	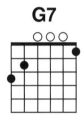		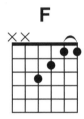	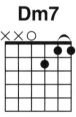

Mandolin

C	F	G7	Em	Dm7
				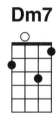

Banjo

C	F	G7	Em	Dm7
	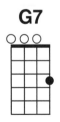	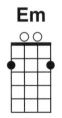		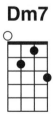

The Circle Game

Words and Music by Joni Mitchell

Verse
Moderately

1. Yes - ter - day a child came out to won - der,
2., 3., 4. *See additional lyrics*

caught a drag - on - fly in - side a jar.

Fear - ful when the sky was full of thun - der and

tear - ful at the fall - ing of a star. And the

Chorus

sea - sons, they go 'round and 'round, and the paint - ed po - nies go up and down.

We're cap - tive on the car - ou - sel of time. We can't re - turn; we can

on - ly look be - hind from where we came and go 'round and 'round and

1., 2., 3.

'round in the cir - cle game.

4. 4. So the game.

Additional Lyrics

2. Then the child moved ten times round the seasons,
Skated over ten clear frozen streams.
Words like "when you're older" must appease him
And promises of someday make his dreams.

3. Sixteen springs and sixteen summers gone now.
Cartwheels turn to car wheels through the town.
And they tell him, "Take your time. It won't be long now
Till you drag your feet to slow the circles down."

4. So the years spin by and now the boy is twenty,
Though his dreams have lost some grandeur coming true.
There'll be new dreams, maybe better dreams and plenty
Before the last revolving year is through.

Standard Ukulele

G	D	Am	C
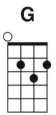	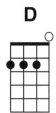	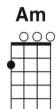	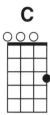

Baritone Ukulele

G	D	Am	C
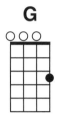		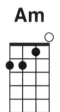	

Guitar

G	D	Am	C
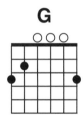	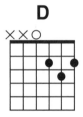		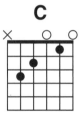

Mandolin

G	D	Am	C
	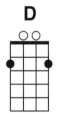		

Banjo

G	D	Am	C
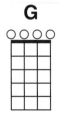	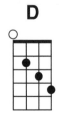		

Closing Time
Words and Music by Dan Wilson

Verse
Moderately

1. Clos-ing time; _ o-pen all the doors _ and let _ you out in - to the world. _
2. See additional lyrics

Clos-ing time; _ turn all of the lights _ on o - ver

ev - 'ry boy and ev - er - y girl. _ Clos-ing time; _

one last call for al - co-hol, _ so fin-ish your whis - key or beer. _

Clos-ing time; _ you don't have to go _ home, but you can't stay _ here. _

Chorus

_ I know who _ I want _ to take me home.

I know who _ I want _ to take me home. I know who _ I want _

_ to take me home, take me _ home. _

Additional Lyrics

2. Closing time; time for you to go out
   To the places you will be from.
   Closing time; this room won't be open
   Till your brothers or your sisters come.
   So gather up your jackets; move it to the exits.
   I hope you have found a friend.
   Closing time; every new beginning
   Comes from some other beginning's end, yeah.

Standard Ukulele

G	C	D	Am	Bm	Amaj7	F

Baritone Ukulele

G	C	D	Am	Bm	Amaj7	F
		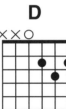				

Guitar

G	C	D	Am	Bm	Amaj7	F
		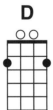				

Mandolin

G	C	D	Am	Bm	Amaj7	F

Banjo

G	C	D	Am	Bm	Amaj7	F

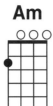

Come Monday
Words and Music by Jimmy Buffett

Verse
Moderately

1. Head-in' up to San Fran-cis - co for the La-bor Day week-end show. _
2., 3. *See additional lyrics*

I've got my Hush _ Pup-pies on; _ I guess I nev-er was meant _ for glit-ter _ rock and roll. _

And hon-ey, I _ did-n't know _ that I'd be miss - in' you so. _ Come

Chorus

Mon-day, it -'ll be all right. _ Come Mon-day, I'll be hold-in' you tight. I spent

four lone-ly days in a brown L. A. haze _ and I just want you back by my side.

Fine **Bridge**

I can't help it, hon-ey. You're that much a part _

_ of me now. _ Re-mem-ber that night _ in Mon-tan - a when we

Interlude *D.C. al Fine*

said there'd be no room for doubt?

Additional Lyrics

2. Yes, it's been quite a summer,
Rent-a-cars and westbound trains.
And now you're off on vacation,
Somethin' you tried to explain.
And darlin', it's I love you so;
That's the reason I just let you go.

3. I hope you're enjoyin' the scenery;
I know that it's pretty up there.
We can go hikin' on Tuesday;
With you I'd walk anywhere.
California has worn me quite thin;
I just can't wait to see you again.

Standard Ukulele

| Em | Bm7 | D7sus4 | C | D | Gmaj7 | F | G |

Baritone Ukulele

| Em | Bm7 | D7sus4 | C | D | Gmaj7 | F | G |

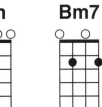    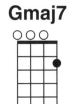  

Guitar

| Em | Bm7 | D7sus4 | C | D | Gmaj7 | F | G |

 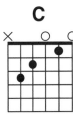 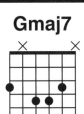 

Mandolin

| Em | Bm7 | D7sus4 | C | D | Gmaj7 | F | G |

   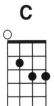 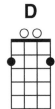  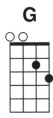

Banjo

| Em | Bm7 | D7sus4 | C | D | Gmaj7 | F | G |

    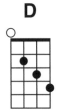   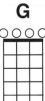

Constant Craving
Words and Music by K.D. Lang and Ben Mink

Verse
Moderately fast

1. E - ven through the ___ dark - est phase,
2. May - be a great ___ mag - net pulls

be it thick or ___ thin, ___ al -
all souls to - wards ___ truth. ___ Or may -

ways some - one ___ march - es brave here be -
be it is ___ life it - self that feeds wis -

Pre-Chorus

- neath my ___ skin. ___ Con - stant crav -
- dom to its youth. ___

ing has al - ways ___ been.

Chorus

Crav - ing. Ah, ha. ___

___ Con - stant crav - ing has al -

- ways ___ been, ___ has al -

- ways ___ been.

Standard Ukulele

D	G	Em	A	Esus4	E	A#°7	Bm
		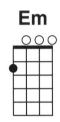	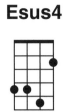				

 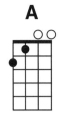  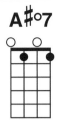 

Baritone Ukulele

D	G	Em	A	Esus4	E	A#°7	Bm
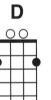	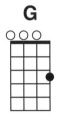						

Guitar

D	G	Em	A	Esus4	E	A#°7	Bm
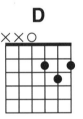	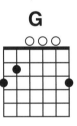	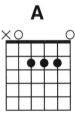		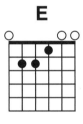	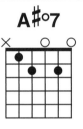		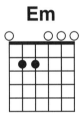

Mandolin

D	G	Em	A	Esus4	E	A#°7	Bm
	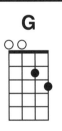	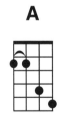			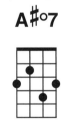	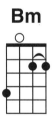	

Banjo

D	G	Em	A	Esus4	E	A#°7	Bm
	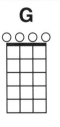	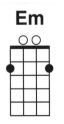		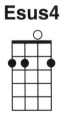		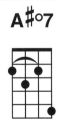	

Dance with Me

Words and Music by John and Johanna Hall

Standard Ukulele

| G | Am | Bm | C | F |

Baritone Ukulele

| G | Am | Bm | C | F |

Guitar

| G | Am | Bm | C | F |

Mandolin

| G | Am | Bm | C | F |

   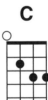

Banjo

| G | Am | Bm | C | F |

Diamonds on the Inside

Words and Music by Ben Harper

Additional Lyrics

2. When you have everything,
   You have everything to lose.
   She made herself a bed of nails
   And she's planning on putting it to use.

3. A candle throws its light into the darkness.
   In a nasty world, so shines a good deed.
   Make sure the fortune that you seek
   Is the fortune that you need.

4. Tell me why the first to ask
   Is the last to give every time.
   What you say and do not mean
   Follows you close behind.

5. Like the soldier long standing under fire,
   Any change comes as a relief.
   Let the giver's name remain unspoken;
   She is just a generous thief.

Standard Ukulele

C	C7	Fmaj7	E+	Am7	D7	G7sus4	G7
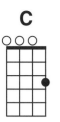	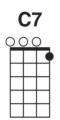	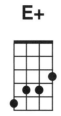	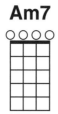		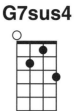	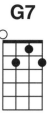	

Baritone Ukulele

C	C7	Fmaj7	E+	Am7	D7	G7sus4	G7
				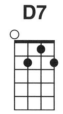	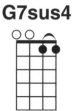		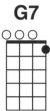

Guitar

C	C7	Fmaj7	E+	Am7	D7	G7sus4	G7
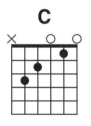	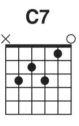	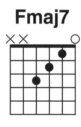	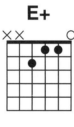	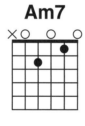		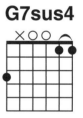	

Mandolin

C	C7	Fmaj7	E+	Am7	D7	G7sus4	G7
				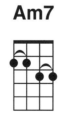	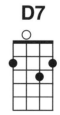	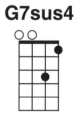	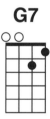

Banjo

C	C7	Fmaj7	E+	Am7	D7	G7sus4	G7
				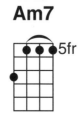			

Don't Know Why

Words and Music by Jesse Harris

Standard Ukulele

Em	D	C	G	G7
	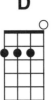			

Baritone Ukulele

Em	D	C	G	G7

Guitar

Em	D	C	G	G7

Mandolin

Em	D	C	G	G7
	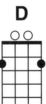			

Banjo

Em	D	C	G	G7

Dream Weaver
Words and Music by Gary Wright

Standard Ukulele

G	C	Am	Dm7	D	Am7	F
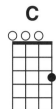	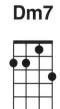	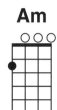		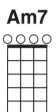	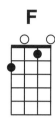	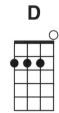

Baritone Ukulele

G	C	Am	Dm7	D	Am7	F
				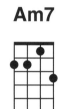		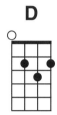

Guitar

G	C	Am	Dm7	D	Am7	F
	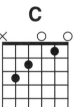		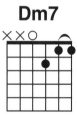	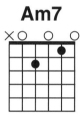		

Mandolin

G	C	Am	Dm7	D	Am7	F
	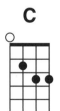				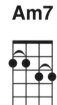	

Banjo

G	C	Am	Dm7	D	Am7	F
			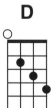		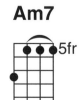	

Dust in the Wind

Words and Music by Kerry Livgren

Standard Ukulele

G	Bm	Am	D7	Gsus4

Baritone Ukulele

G	Bm	Am	D7	Gsus4

Guitar

G	Bm	Am	D7	Gsus4

Mandolin

G	Bm	Am	D7	Gsus4

Banjo

G	Bm	Am	D7	Gsus4

Early Mornin' Rain
Words and Music by Gordon Lightfoot

Moderately, in 2

Chorus

1. In the ear - ly morn - in' rain, with a dol- lar in my hand and an ach - in' in my heart and my pock - ets full of sands. I'm a long way from home and I miss my loved ones so, in the ear - ly morn - in' rain with no place to go.

2., 3., 4. *See additional lyrics*

1., 2., 3.

2. Out on run - way num - ber
3. Hear the might - y en - gine
4. This old air - port's got me

4.

So I'd best be on my way in the ear - ly morn - in' rain.

Additional Lyrics

2. Out on runway number nine,
   Big seven-o-seven set to go,
   But I'm out here on the grass,
   Where the pavement never grows.
   Well, the liquor tasted good
   And the women all were fast.
   There she goes my friend;
   She's rollin' down at last.

3. Hear the mighty engine roar,
   See the silver wing on high.
   She's away and westward bound;
   Far above the clouds she'll fly,
   Where the mornin' rain don't fall
   And the sun always shines.
   She'll be flyin' o'er my home
   In about three hours time.

4. This old airport's got me down;
   It's no earthly good to me
   'Cause I'm stuck here on the ground,
   Cold and drunk as I might be.
   You can't jump a jet plane
   Like you can a freight train,
   So I'd best be on my way
   In the early mornin' rain.

Standard Ukulele

Em	F#m	G	D	C

Baritone Ukulele

Em	F#m	G	D	C

Guitar

Em	F#m	G	D	C

Mandolin

Em	F#m	G	D	C

Banjo

Em	F#m	G	D	C

Eight Miles High

Words and Music by Roger McGuinn, David Crosby and Gene Clark

Standard Ukulele

D	Dmaj7	D7	D6	Em7	A7

Baritone Ukulele

D	Dmaj7	D7	D6	Em7	A7

Guitar

D	Dmaj7	D7	D6	Em7	A7

Mandolin

D	Dmaj7	D7	D6	Em7	A7

   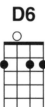

Banjo

D	Dmaj7	D7	D6	Em7	A7

Everybody's Talkin'
(Echoes)
from MIDNIGHT COWBOY
Words and Music by Fred Neil

Verse
Moderately fast

Standard Ukulele

Am   **C**   **F**   **G**   **E**

Baritone Ukulele

Am   **C**   **F**   **G**   **E**

Guitar

Am   **C**  **F**   **G**   **E**

Mandolin

Am   **C**   **F**   **G**   **E**

Banjo

Am   **C**   **F**   **G**   **E**

Flake

Words and Music by Jack Johnson

Verse
Moderately

1. I know she said, "It's all _____ right, you will make it up next time." _
2. *See additional lyrics*

I know she knows it's not _____ right. There ain't no use in lyin'. _

May-be she thinks I know _____ some-thin'. May-be, may-be she thinks _ it's fine.

Or may-be she knows some-thin' _____ I don't. I'm so, I'm so tired. _

Chorus

I'm so tired of try-in'. It seems to me that "may - be," _____

it pret-ty much al-ways means _____ "no." So don't _____ tell me _____ you

might just let _____ it go. _____ But of-ten times we're la-

- zy. _ It seems to stand in my _____ way, _ 'cause no one, no, _ not no _

— one likes to be let down. _

Additional Lyrics

2. I know she loves the sunrise; no longer sees it with her sleeping eyes.
   And I know that when she said she's gonna try, well, it might not work because of other ties.
   And I know she usually has some other ties, and I wouldn't wanna break 'em now. I wouldn't wanna break 'em.
   Maybe she'll help me to untie this, but until then, well, I'm gonna have to lie too.

Standard Ukulele

E	A	D
		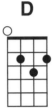

Baritone Ukulele

E	A	D

Guitar

E	A	D

Mandolin

E	A	D

Banjo

E	A	D

For What It's Worth

Words and Music by Stephen Stills

**Verse
Moderately**

1. There's some-thing hap-pen-ing here, ___ but what it
2., 3., 4. *See additional lyrics*

is ain't ex-act-ly clear. ___ There's a man with a gun o-ver there ___

___ tell-ing me I've got to be-ware. ___ I think it's time we

stop; chil-dren, what's that sound? __ Ev-'ry-bod-y look what's go-ing down. ___

Fine   **1., 2.**   **3.   D.C. al Fine**

___

Additional Lyrics

2. There's battle lines being drawn.
   Nobody's right if everybody's wrong.
   Young people speaking their minds,
   Getting so much resistance from behind.
   I think it's time we stop; hey, what's that sound?
   Everybody look what's going down.

3. What a field day for the heat.
   A thousand people in the street,
   Singing songs and carrying signs,
   Mostly say, "Hooray for our side."
   It's time we stop; hey, what's that sound?
   Everybody look what's going down.

4. Paranoia strikes deep.
   Into your life it will creep.
   It starts when you're always afraid.
   You step out of line, the man come and take you away.
   We better stop; hey, what's that sound?
   Everybody look what's going down.

Standard Ukulele

E

Asus2

Bsus4

Baritone Ukulele

E

Asus2

Bsus4

Guitar

E

Asus2

Bsus4

Mandolin

E

Asus2

Bsus4

Banjo

E

Asus2

Bsus4

Free Fallin'

Words and Music by Tom Petty and Jeff Lynne

Standard Ukulele

C	G	D	Am	Em	G7
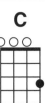	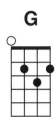	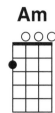	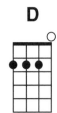		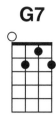

Baritone Ukulele

C	G	D	Am	Em	G7
	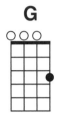			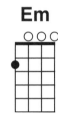	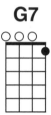

Guitar

C	G	D	Am	Em	G7
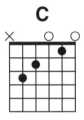	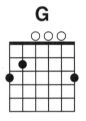	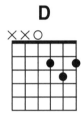	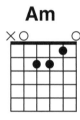		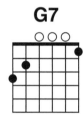

Mandolin

C	G	D	Am	Em	G7
	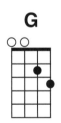	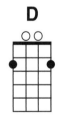	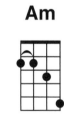		

Banjo

C	G	D	Am	Em	G7
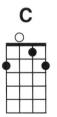	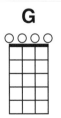	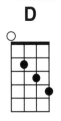		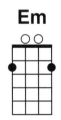	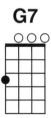

Fugitive

Words and Music by Robbie Malone, Keith Prior and David Gray

Verse
Moderately slow, in 2

Standard Ukulele

D	A7	G	Bm	Esus4	E	C	A

 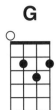 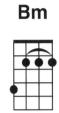   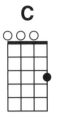 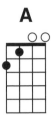

Baritone Ukulele

D	A7	G	Bm	Esus4	E	C	A

 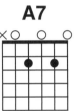 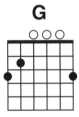   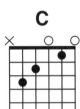 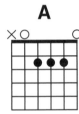

Guitar

D	A7	G	Bm	Esus4	E	C	A

   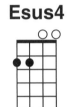 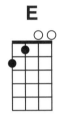 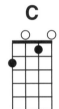 

Mandolin

D	A7	G	Bm	Esus4	E	C	A

  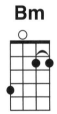  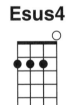  

Banjo

D	A7	G	Bm	Esus4	E	C	A

  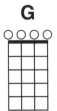 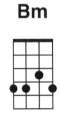 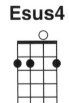 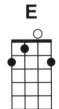 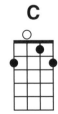 

Give a Little Bit

Words and Music by Rick Davies and Roger Hodgson

Standard Ukulele

G	C	D	Em
	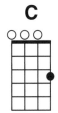	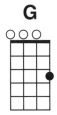	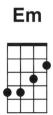

Baritone Ukulele

G	C	D	Em
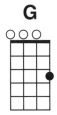	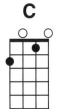	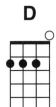	

Guitar

G	C	D	Em
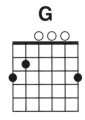	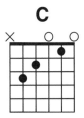		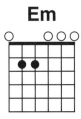

Mandolin

G	C	D	Em
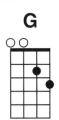	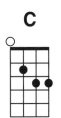	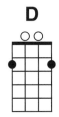	

Banjo

G	C	D	Em
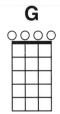	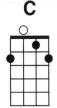	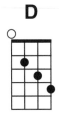	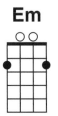

Good Riddance
(Time of Your Life)
Words by Billie Joe
Music by Green Day

Verse
Moderately, in 2

1. An - oth - er turn - ing point, a fork stuck in the road.
2. So take the pho - to - graphs and still frames in your mind.

Time grabs you by the wrist, di - rects
Hang it on a shelf in good

you where to go.
health and good time.

So make the best of this test
Tat - toos of mem - o - ries and dead

and don't ask why.
skin on trial.

It's not a ques -
For what it's worth,

- tion, but a les - son learned in time.
it was worth all the while.

It's

Chorus

some - thing un - pre - dict - a - ble, but in the end it's right.

I hope you had the time of your life.

Standard Ukulele

C   Am   F   G   Em

Baritone Ukulele

C   Am   F   G   Em

Guitar

C   Am   F   G   Em

Mandolin

C   Am   F   G   Em

Banjo

C   Am   F   G   Em

Hallelujah

Words and Music by Leonard Cohen

Standard Ukulele

C	Am7	Fsus2	G	Am	Em	G7sus4	F

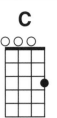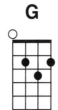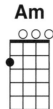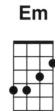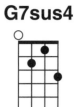

Baritone Ukulele

C	Am7	Fsus2	G	Am	Em	G7sus4	F

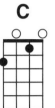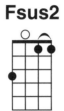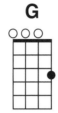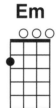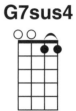

Guitar

C	Am7	Fsus2	G	Am	Em	G7sus4	F

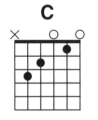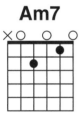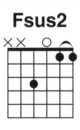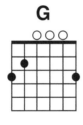

Mandolin

C	Am7	Fsus2	G	Am	Em	G7sus4	F

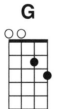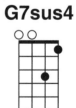

Banjo

C	Am7	Fsus2	G	Am	Em	G7sus4	F

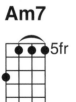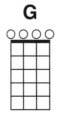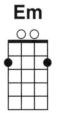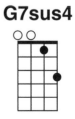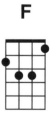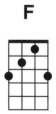

Have a Little Faith in Me

Words and Music by John Hiatt

Verse
Moderately

1. When the road gets dark ___ and you ___ can no long-er
2., 3., 4. *See additional lyrics*

see, ___ just let my love ___ throw a spark, ___

and have a lit-tle faith in ___ me. ___ And have a lit-tle

Chorus

faith in ___ me, ___ have a lit-tle faith in ___ me.

And have a lit-tle faith in ___ me, ___ have a lit-tle

To Coda ⊕ **D.C. al Coda (take repeat)** ⊕ **Coda**

faith in ___ me. ___

Additional Lyrics

2. And when the tears you cry
   Are all you can believe,
   Just give these loving arms a try, baby,
   And have a little faith in me.

3. When your secret heart
   Cannot speak so easily,
   Come here, darlin'; from a whisper, start
   To have a little faith in me.

4. And when your back's against the wall,
   Just turn around and you, you will see.
   I will catch you, I will catch your fall, baby.
   Just have a little faith in me.

Standard Ukulele

C	G	F	Am
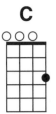	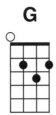	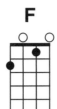	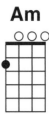

Baritone Ukulele

C	G	F	Am
	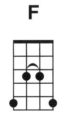	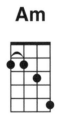	

Guitar

C	G	F	Am
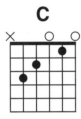	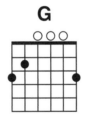	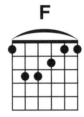	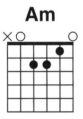

Mandolin

C	G	F	Am
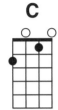	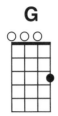		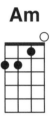

Banjo

C	G	F	Am
	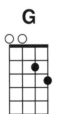		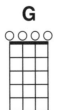

Have You Ever Seen the Rain?

Words and Music by John Fogerty

Standard Ukulele

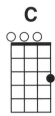
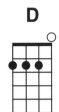

Baritone Ukulele

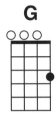

Guitar

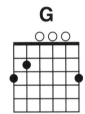
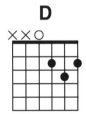
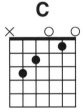

Mandolin

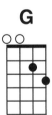
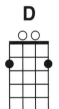
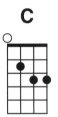

Banjo

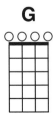

Hickory Wind

Words and Music by Gram Parsons and Bob Buchanan

Verse

Standard Ukulele

| G | Bm | Em | C | D7 | D | F |

Baritone Ukulele

| G | Bm | Em | C | D7 | D | F |

Guitar

| G | Bm | Em | C | D7 | D | F |

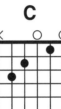

Mandolin

| G | Bm | Em | C | D7 | D | F |

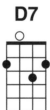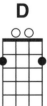

Banjo

| G | Bm | Em | C | D7 | D | F |

Hold You in My Arms

Words and Music by Ray LaMontagne and Ethan Johns

Verse
Moderately slow, in 2

1. When you came to me with your bad dreams and your fears,
2., 3. *See additional lyrics*

was eas - y to see you'd been cry - ing.

Seems like ev - 'ry - where you turn, ca - tas - tro - phe reigns.

But who real - ly prof - its from the dy - ing?

Chorus

I could hold you in my arms. I could

hold { you / you / on } for - ev - er. And I could

hold you in my arms, oh. I could

hold { you / you / on } for - ev - er.

Additional Lyrics

2. When you kissed my lips
   With my mouth so full of questions,
   My worried mind, that you quiet.
   Place your hands on my face,
   Close my eyes and say
   That love is a poor man's food, no prophesying.

3. So now we see how it is;
   This fist begets the spear.
   Weapons of war, symptoms of madness.
   Don't let your eyes refuse to see,
   Don't let your ears refuse to hear.
   You ain't never gonna shake this sense of sadness.

Standard Ukulele

Em   **D6**

Baritone Ukulele

Em   **D6**

Guitar

Em   **D6**

Mandolin

Em   **D6**

Banjo

Em   **D6**

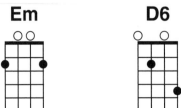

A Horse with No Name

Words and Music by Dewey Bunnell

Standard Ukulele

C 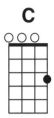 **F**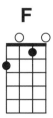

Baritone Ukulele

C  **F**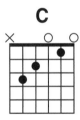

Guitar

C  **F**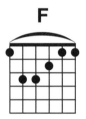

Mandolin

C  **F**

Banjo

C  **F**

I Melt with You

Words and Music by Richard Ian Brown, Michael Francis Conroy, Robert James Grey, Gary Frances McDowell and Stephen James Walker

Standard Ukulele

C	Am	F	G	E	Fm
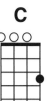	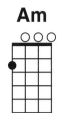	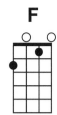			

Baritone Ukulele

C	Am	F	G	E	Fm
			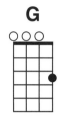	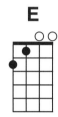	

Guitar

C	Am	F	G	E	Fm
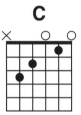				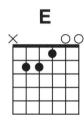	

Mandolin

C	Am	F	G	E	Fm
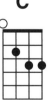	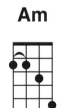		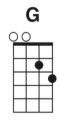		

Banjo

C	Am	F	G	E	Fm
			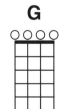	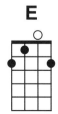	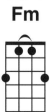

I Will Follow You Into the Dark

Words and Music by Benjamin Gibbard

Verse
Moderately slow, in 2

1. Love of ___ mine, ___ some-day you will ___ die, ___ but I'll be close be-hind.
2., 3. *See additional lyrics*

I'll fol-low you ___ in-to the dark. ___ No blind-ing ___ light ___ or tun-nels to

gates of ___ white, ___ just our hands clasped so ___ tight, ___ wait-ing for ___ the hint of a

To Coda 1 ⊕

𝄋 Chorus

spark. If heav-en and hell de-cide ___ that they both ___ are sat-is-fied, ___ il-

lu-mi-nate the "No's" ___ on their va - can - cy signs; ___ if there's no one be-side ___

To Coda 2 ⊕

___ you when your soul ___ em - barks, ___ then I'll fol - low you ___ in - to ___ the dark.

2nd time,
D.C. al Coda 1

2. In

⊕ Coda 1

soon in the black - est ___ of rooms.

D.S. al Coda 2

If

⊕ Coda 2

Then I'll fol - low you ___ in-to ___ the dark.

Additional Lyrics

2. In Catholic school, as vicious as Roman rule,
I got my knuckles bruised by a lady in black.
I held my tongue as she told me, "Son,
Fear is the heart of love."
So I never went back.

3. You and me have seen everything to see,
From Bangkok to Calgary. And the soles of your shoes
Are all worn down. The time for sleep is now,
But it's nothing to cry about,
'Cause we'll hold each other… *(To Coda 1)*

Standard Ukulele

A	Amaj7	D	E

Baritone Ukulele

A	Amaj7	D	E

Guitar

A	Amaj7	D	E

Mandolin

A	Amaj7	D	E

Banjo

A	Amaj7	D	E
	2fr		

I Wonder

Words and Music by Sixto Diaz Rodriguez

Additional Lyrics

2. I wonder about the love you can't find,
   And I wonder about the loneliness that's mine.
   I wonder how much going have you got,
   And I wonder about your friends that are not.
   I wonder, I wonder, wonder, I do.

3. I wonder about the tears in children's eyes,
   And I wonder about the soldier that dies.
   I wonder, will this hatred ever end?
   I wonder and worry, my friend.
   I wonder, I wonder, wonder, don't you?

4. I wonder how many times you've been had,
   And I wonder how many dreams have gone bad.
   I wonder how many times you've had sex,
   And I wonder, do you know who'll be next?
   I wonder, I wonder, wonder, I do.

Standard Ukulele

C	D	Em	G	Am7
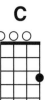	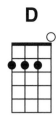	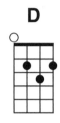	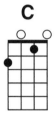	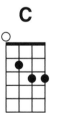

Baritone Ukulele

C	D	Em	G	Am7
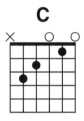	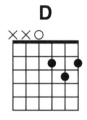	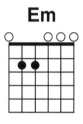	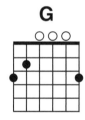	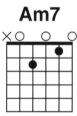

Guitar

C	D	Em	G	Am7
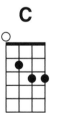	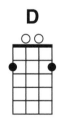		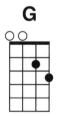	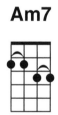

Mandolin

C	D	Em	G	Am7
	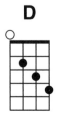	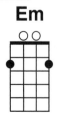	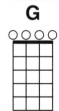	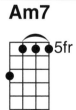

Banjo

Ice Cream

Words and Music by Sarah McLachlan

Standard Ukulele

G	Am	C	Em	D

Baritone Ukulele

G	Am	C	Em	D

Guitar

G	Am	C	Em	D

Mandolin

G	Am	C	Em	D

Banjo

G	Am	C	Em	D

Iris

from the Motion Picture CITY OF ANGELS
Words and Music by John Rzeznik

Additional Lyrics

2. And all I can taste is this moment,
And all I can breathe is your life.
And sooner or later it's over.
I just don't wanna miss you tonight.

3. And you can't fight the tears that ain't coming
Or the moment of truth in your lies.
When everything feels like the movies,
Yeah, you bleed just to know you're alive.

Standard Ukulele

C	Em	F	G	Am
  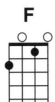 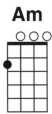

Baritone Ukulele

C	Em	F	G	Am

Guitar

C	Em	F	G	Am

Mandolin

C	Em	F	G	Am

Banjo

C	Em	F	G	Am

It's a Heartache
Words and Music by Ronnie Scott and Steve Wolfe

Standard Ukulele

G	F	C	Dm
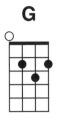	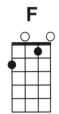	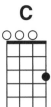	

Baritone Ukulele

G	F	C	Dm
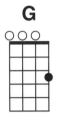		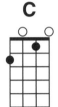	

Guitar

G	F	C	Dm
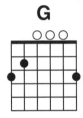		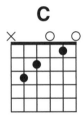	

Mandolin

G	F	C	Dm
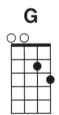			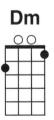

Banjo

G	F	C	Dm
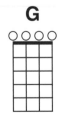			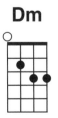

Jealousy
Words and Music by Natalie Merchant

Standard Ukulele

G	D	Am	C
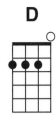	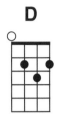		

Standard Ukulele
G   D   Am   C

Baritone Ukulele
G   D   Am   C

Guitar
G   D   Am   C

Mandolin
G   D   Am   C

Banjo
G   D   Am   C

Knockin' on Heaven's Door

Words and Music by Bob Dylan

Verse
Moderately slow

1. Ma - ma, take this badge _____ off of me. ____
2. Ma - ma, put my guns _____ in the ground. ____

I cant use it an - y - more. _____
I can't shoot them ____ an - y - more. ____

It's get - tin' dark, ___ too dark ___ to see. ____
That long black cloud ___ is com - in' down. ____

I feel I'm knock - in" on heav - en's door. ____

Chorus

Knock, knock, knock - in' on heav - en's door. ____

Knock, knock, knock - in' on heav - en's door. ____

Knock, knock, knock - in' on heav - en's door. ____

Knock, knock, knock - in' on heav - en's door. ____

Standard Ukulele

G 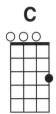 **C** 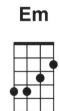 **Em** 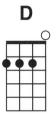 **D**

Baritone Ukulele

G 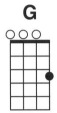 **C** 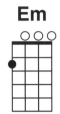 **Em** 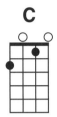 **D**

Guitar

G 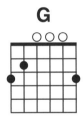 **C** 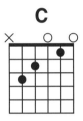 **Em**  **D**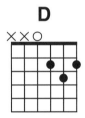

Mandolin

G 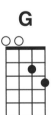 **C**  **Em**  **D**

Banjo

G 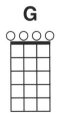 **C** 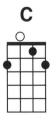 **Em** 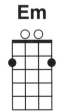 **D**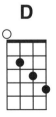

Leaving on a Jet Plane

Words and Music by John Denver

Standard Ukulele

G	Em	Bm	D	C	Am

Baritone Ukulele

G	Em	Bm	D	C	Am

Guitar

G	Em	Bm	D	C	Am

Mandolin

G	Em	Bm	D	C	Am

Banjo

G	Em	Bm	D	C	Am

Lonely People

Words and Music by Dan Peek and Catherine L. Peek

Standard Ukulele

| Cmaj7 | Dm7 | F | Em | Dm | G7sus4 | A |

Baritone Ukulele

| Cmaj7 | Dm7 | F | Em | Dm | G7sus4 | A |

Guitar

| Cmaj7 | Dm7 | F | Em | Dm | G7sus4 | A |

Mandolin

| Cmaj7 | Dm7 | F | Em | Dm | G7sus4 | A |

5fr 7fr

Banjo

| Cmaj7 | Dm7 | F | Em | Dm | G7sus4 | A |

Make It with You
Words and Music by David Gates

Verse
Moderately slow, in 2

1. Hey, have you ev - er tried
2. No, you don't know me well,

real - ly reach-ing out for the oth - er side?
and ev - 'ry lit - tle thing on - ly time will tell.

I may be climb - ing on rain - bows, but,
But you be - lieve the things that I do, and

ba - by, here goes. Dreams,
we'll see it through. Life

they're for those who sleep. Life is for
can be short or long. Love can be

us to keep. And if you're won - d'ring what this all is
right or wrong. And if I chose the one I'd like to

lead - ing to, I want ⎱ to make it with you.
help me through, I'd like ⎰

I real - ly think that we could make it, girl.

1. F Em Dm G7sus4
2. G7sus4 Cmaj7

Standard Ukulele

| C | Dm | G | F | Em | Am | D |

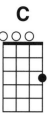 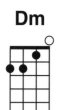 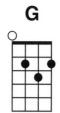 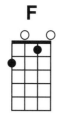 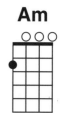  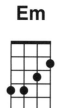

Baritone Ukulele

| C | Dm | G | F | Em | Am | D |

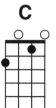  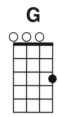  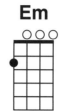 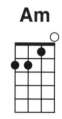 

Guitar

| C | Dm | G | F | Em | Am | D |

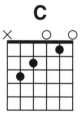 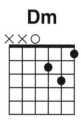   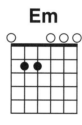 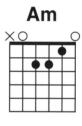 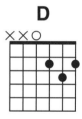

Mandolin

| C | Dm | G | F | Em | Am | D |

 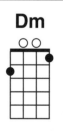 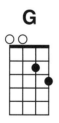   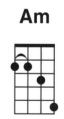 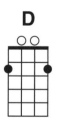

Banjo

| C | Dm | G | F | Em | Am | D |

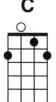 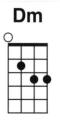 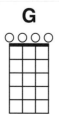 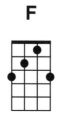 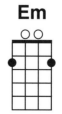  

Morning Has Broken

Words by Eleanor Farjeon
Music by Cat Stevens

Standard Ukulele

D	C	G	Dm	Em7	A
	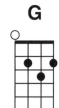	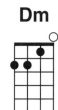		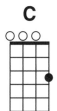	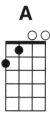

Baritone Ukulele

D	C	G	Dm	Em7	A
		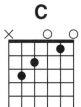	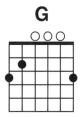		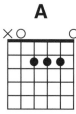

Guitar

D	C	G	Dm	Em7	A
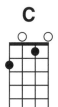	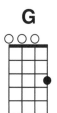	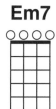	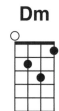	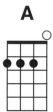	

Mandolin

D	C	G	Dm	Em7	A
		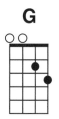	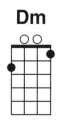	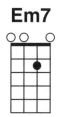	

Banjo

D	C	G	Dm	Em7	A
	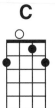	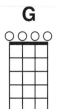	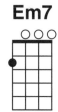	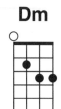	

Norwegian Wood
(This Bird Has Flown)
Words and Music by John Lennon and Paul McCartney

Standard Ukulele

Am	F	C	G	Gsus4
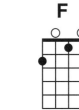	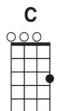	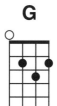		

Baritone Ukulele

Am	F	C	G	Gsus4
	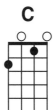	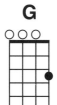	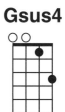	

Guitar

Am	F	C	G	Gsus4
	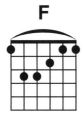			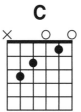

Mandolin

Am	F	C	G	Gsus4
	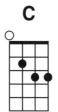	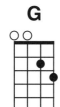		|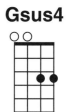

Banjo

Am	F	C	G	Gsus4

One of Us
Words and Music by Eric Bazilian

Standard Ukulele

D	G	A	Em	Dsus4

Baritone Ukulele

D	G	A	Em	Dsus4

Guitar

D	G	A	Em	Dsus4
		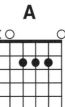		

Mandolin

D	G	A	Em	Dsus4
	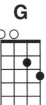		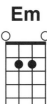	

Banjo

D	G	A	Em	Dsus4

Peaceful Easy Feeling

Words and Music by Jack Tempchin

Standard Ukulele

C	G	F	D	Am
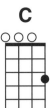	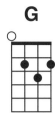	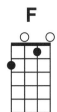		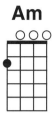

Baritone Ukulele

C	G	F	D	Am
				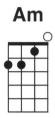

Guitar

C	G	F	D	Am
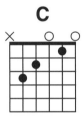	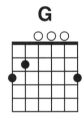	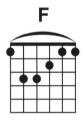	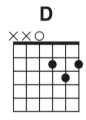	

Mandolin

C	G	F	D	Am
	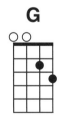		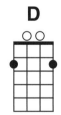	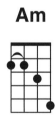

Banjo

C	G	F	D	Am
	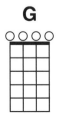		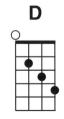	

Reason to Believe

Words and Music by Tim Hardin

Standard Ukulele

G	Em	C	Am	D

Baritone Ukulele

G	Em	C	Am	D

Guitar

G	Em	C	Am	D

Mandolin

G	Em	C	Am	D

Banjo

G	Em	C	Am	D
	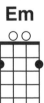			

Redemption Song

Words and Music by Bob Marley

Standard Ukulele

Bm7	G	D	Dsus2	A	Dmaj7	D6

Baritone Ukulele

Bm7	G	D	Dsus2	A	Dmaj7	D6

 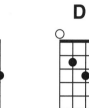  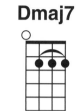

Guitar

Bm7	G	D	Dsus2	A	Dmaj7	D6

Mandolin

Bm7	G	D	Dsus2	A	Dmaj7	D6

  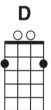

Banjo

Bm7	G	D	Dsus2	A	Dmaj7	D6

The Scientist

Words and Music by Guy Berryman, Jon Buckland, Will Champion and Chris Martin

Verse
Moderately slow

1. Come up to meet you, tell you I'm sorry. You don't know how love-
Tell me your secrets and ask me your questions. Oh, let's go back
2. *See additional lyrics*

-ly you are. I had to find you, tell you I need
to the start. Running in circles, coming up tails,

you, tell you I'll set you apart.
heads on a silence apart.

Chorus

No-body said

it was easy. It's such a shame for us to part.

No-body said it was easy. No one ever

To Coda

said it would be this hard. Oh, take me back to the start.

D.C. al Coda (take repeat)

Coda

said it would be so hard.

I'm going back to the start.

Additional Lyrics

2. I was just guessing at numbers and figures, pulling your puzzles apart.
Questions of science, science and progress that must speak as loud as my heart.
Tell me you love me; come back and haunt me. Oh, and I rush to the start.
Running in circles, chasing our tails, coming back as we are.

Standard Ukulele

C	Am	Dm	G	Fmaj7	Em	F	G#°7

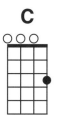 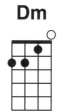 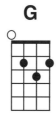     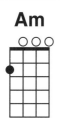

Baritone Ukulele

C	Am	Dm	G	Fmaj7	Em	F	G#°7

  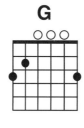   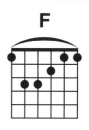 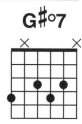 

Guitar

C	Am	Dm	G	Fmaj7	Em	F	G#°7

  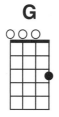  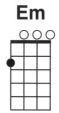   

Mandolin

C	Am	Dm	G	Fmaj7	Em	F	G#°7

 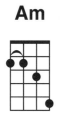 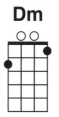  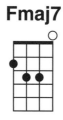   

Banjo

C	Am	Dm	G	Fmaj7	Em	F	G#°7

  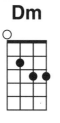 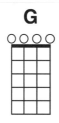 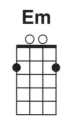 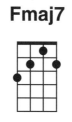  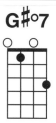

Sky Blue Sky

Words and Music by Jeff Tweedy

Verse
Moderately

1. Oh, the band marched on in for-ma - tion.
2. *See additional lyrics*

The brass was phas - ing tunes I could-n't place.

Win - dows o - pen and rain - ing in

ma - roon, yel - low, blue, gold and gray.

1. 2. The

2.

Chorus

With a sky blue sky, this rot - ten time

would-n't seem so bad to me now.

Oh, I did-n't die. I should be sat - is - fied. I sur - vived;

that's good e - nough for now.

Additional Lyrics

2. The drunks were ricocheting.
   The old buildings downtown, empty so long ago.
   Windows broken and dreaming,
   So happy to leave what was my home.

Standard Ukulele

G	Em	D	C	C7

Baritone Ukulele

G	Em	D	C	C7

Guitar

G	Em	D	C	C7

Mandolin

G	Em	D	C	C7

Banjo

G	Em	D	C	C7

Slip Slidin' Away

Words and Music by Paul Simon

Additional Lyrics

2. And I know a woman; became a wife.
   These are the very words she uses to describe her life.
   She said, "A good day ain't got no rain."
   She said, "A bad day's when I lie in bed and think of things that might have been."

3. And I know a father who had a son.
   He longed to tell him all the reasons for the things he'd done.
   He came a long way just to explain.
   He kissed his boy as he lay sleeping, then he turned around and headed home again.

4. God only knows; God makes His plan.
   The information's unavailable to the mortal man.
   We're workin' our jobs, collect our pay,
   Believe we're glidin' down the highway when, in fact, we're slip slidin' away.

Standard Ukulele

  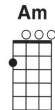   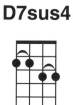

C G Am Em D D7sus4

Baritone Ukulele

 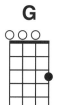 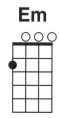 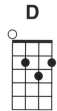 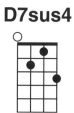

C G Am Em D D7sus4

Guitar

 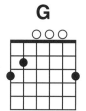    

C G Am Em D D7sus4

Mandolin

 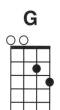  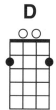 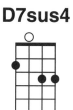

C G Am Em D D7sus4

Banjo

 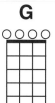

C G Am Em D D7sus4

5fr

Songbird

Words and Music by Christine McVie

Standard Ukulele

G	Am	F	C
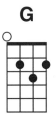	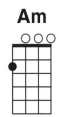	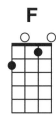	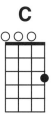

Baritone Ukulele

G	Am	F	C
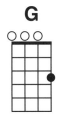			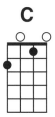

Guitar

G	Am	F	C
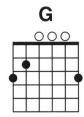	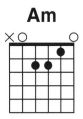		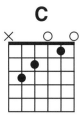

Mandolin

G	Am	F	C
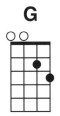	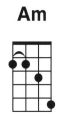	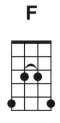	

Banjo

G	Am	F	C
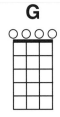			

The Sound of Silence

Words and Music by Paul Simon

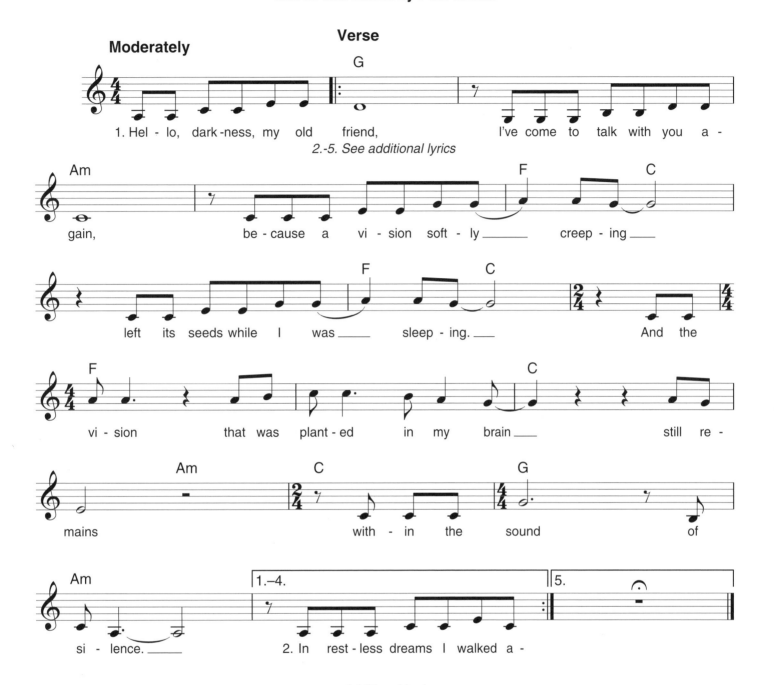

Moderately

Verse

1. Hel - lo, dark -ness, my old friend, I've come to talk with you a -

2.-5. See additional lyrics

gain, be - cause a vi - sion soft - ly creep - ing

left its seeds while I was sleep - ing. And the

vi - sion that was plant - ed in my brain still re -

mains with - in the sound of

si - lence.

1.–4. 2. In rest - less dreams I walked a -

5.

Additional Lyrics

2. In restless dreams I walked alone,
Narrow streets of cobblestone.
'Neath the halo of a streetlamp,
I turned my collar to the cold and damp,
When my eyes were stabbed by the flash
Of a neon light
That split the night and touched the
Sound of silence.

3. And in the naked light I saw
Ten thousand people, maybe more.
People talking without speaking,
People hearing without listening,
People writing songs that voices never share,
And no one dare disturb the sound of silence.

4. "Fools!" said I, "You do not know.
Silence like a cancer grows.
Hear my words that I might teach you.
Take my arms that I might reach you."
But my words, like silent raindrops fell
And echoed in the wells of silence.

5. And the people bowed and prayed
To the neon god they made.
And the sign flashed out its warning
In the words that it was forming.
And the sign said, "The words of the
Prophets are
Written on the subway walls and
Tenement halls."
Whisper the sounds of silence.

Standard Ukulele

E

A6

B6

Baritone Ukulele

E

A6

B6

Guitar

E

A6

B6

Mandolin

E

A6

B6

Banjo

E

A6

B6

Steal My Kisses

Words and Music by Ben Harper

Verse
Moderate Reggae

1. I pulled in to Nash - ville, Ten - nes - see, ___ but
2., 3. *See additional lyrics*

you would - n't e - ven come ___ a - round ___ to see me. ___ And

since you're head - ing up ___ to Car - o - li - na, you

know I'm gon - na be right ___ there ___ be - hind ___ ya. 'Cause I

Chorus

al - ways have ___ to steal ___ my kiss - es from you. ___ I

al - ways have ___ to steal ___ my kiss - es from you.

Al - ways have ___ to steal ___ my kiss - es from ___ you. I

al - ways have ___ to steal ___ my kiss - es from ___ you. ___

2. Now, I'd ___ you. ___
3. Now,

Additional Lyrics

2. Now, I'd love to feel that warm southern rain.
   Just to hear it fall is the sweetest sounding thing.
   And to see it fall on your simple country dress,
   It's like heaven to me, I must confess.

3. Now, I've been hanging 'round you for days,
   But when I lean in, you just turn your head away.
   Whoa, no, you didn't mean that.
   She said, "I love the way you think but I hate the way you act."

Standard Ukulele

G	D7	Em	C	Gsus4

Baritone Ukulele

G	D7	Em	C	Gsus4

Guitar

G	D7	Em	C	Gsus4

Mandolin

G	D7	Em	C	Gsus4
	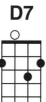			

Banjo

G	D7	Em	C	Gsus4

The Story

Words and Music by Phil Hanseroth

Additional Lyrics

2. I climbed across the mountaintops,
Swam all across the ocean blue.
I crossed all the lines and I broke all the rules,
But, baby, I broke them all for you.
Oh, because even when I was flat broke,
You made me feel like a million bucks. You do.
I was made for you.

3. You see the smile that's on my mouth?
It's hiding the words that don't come out.
All of my friends who think that I'm blessed,
They don't know my head is a mess.
No, they don't know who I really am,
And they don't know what I've been through like you do.
And I was made for you.

Standard Ukulele

E G D A Am7 Bm7 Em7 B7sus4

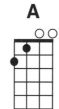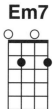

Baritone Ukulele

E G D A Am7 Bm7 Em7 B7sus4

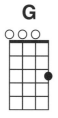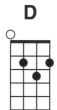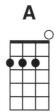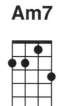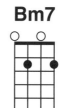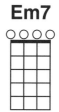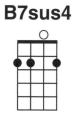

Guitar

E G D A Am7 Bm7 Em7 B7sus4

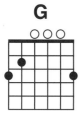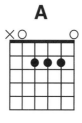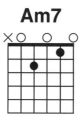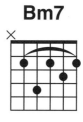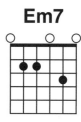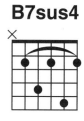

Mandolin

E G D A Am7 Bm7 Em7 B7sus4

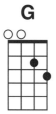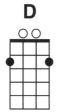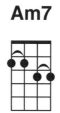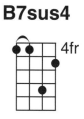

Banjo

E G D A Am7 Bm7 Em7 B7sus4

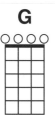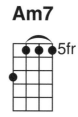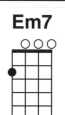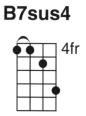

Summer Breeze
Words and Music by James Seals and Dash Crofts

Standard Ukulele

A	E	D	G	Dmaj7	D6	C#m	Bm

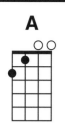  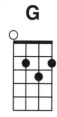 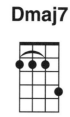  

Baritone Ukulele

A	E	D	G	Dmaj7	D6	C#m	Bm

 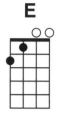  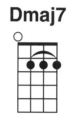  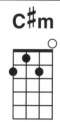 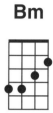

Guitar

A	E	D	G	Dmaj7	D6	C#m	Bm

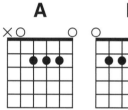 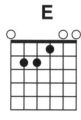 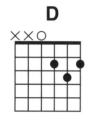 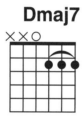 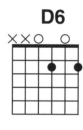 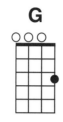 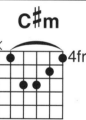 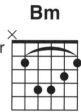

4fr

Mandolin

A	E	D	G	Dmaj7	D6	C#m	Bm

  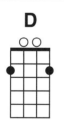     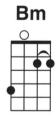

Banjo

A	E	D	G	Dmaj7	D6	C#m	Bm

 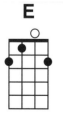 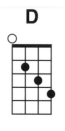 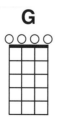   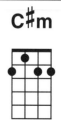 

Sunshine
(Go Away Today)

Words and Music by Jonathan Edwards

Verse
Moderately fast

1., 3. Sun - shine, go ___ a - way to - day; ___ I don't feel much ___ like
2., 4., 5. *See additional lyrics*

danc - in'. ___ Some man's gone ___ and he's tried to run my ___ life. ___ He

don't know what ___ he's ___ ask - in'. 2. When

Chorus

How much does it ___ cost? I'll buy ___ it. The time is all ___ we've ___ lost;

I'll try ___ it. And he can't e - ven run ___ his own ___ life. ___ I'll be

damned if he'll ___ run mine! ___ Sun - shine. ___ Sun - shine. ___

Instrumental…

Additional Lyrics

2. When he tells me I better get in line,
   Can't hear what he's sayin'.
   When I grow up, I'm gonna make it mine.
   These ain't dues I been payin'.

4. Working starts to make me wonder where
   Fruits of what I do are goin'.
   When he says in love and war all is fair,
   He's got cards he ain't showin'.

5. Sunshine, come on back another day;
   I promise you I'll be singin'.
   This old world, she's gonna turn around,
   Brand new bells will be ringin'.

Standard Ukulele

C7 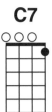   **F**    **G**

Baritone Ukulele

C7   **F**    **G**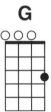

Guitar

C7   **F** 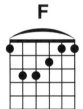   **G**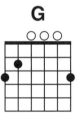

Mandolin

C7   **F**   **G**

Banjo

C7   **F**   **G**

Sunshine Superman

Words and Music by Donovan Leitch

Verse
Moderately

C7

1. Sun - shine _ came soft - ly through my win - dow to - day. _
2., 3. *See additional lyrics*

Could have tripped out eas - y, but I've, I changed my way. _

F

It - 'll take time, _ I know _ it, but in a while, _

C7

you're gon - na be mine _ and I know it. We'll do it in style. _

Chorus

G   F

1. 'Cause I've made my mind up; you're go - ing to be mine. _ I'll tell you right now,
2., 3. When you've made your mind up for - ev - er to be mine, _ mm, _

C7

an - y trick in the book, _ a now, ba - by, all that I can find.
I'll pick up your hand _ and _ slow - ly blow your lit - tle mind. _

Fine G   F

_ 'Cause I've made my mind up; you're go - ing to be mine. _ I'll tell you right now,

**D.C. al Fine
(no repeat)**

C7

an - y trick in the book, _ a now, ba - by, all that I can find. _

Additional Lyrics

2. Everybody's hustlin' just to have a little scene.
   When I said we'd be cool, I think that you know what I mean.
   We stood on a beach at sunset. Do you remember when?
   I know a beach where, baby, it never ends.

3. Superman or Green Lantern ain't got nothin' on me.
   I can make like a turtle and dive for pearls in the sea.
   You can just sit there while thinkin' on your velvet throne.
   I've followed the rainbow so you can have all your own.

Standard Ukulele

G	D	Em	C
	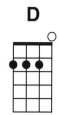		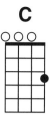

Baritone Ukulele

G	D	Em	C
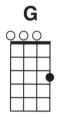		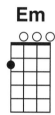	

Guitar

G	D	Em	C
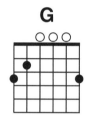	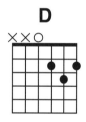	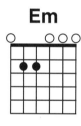	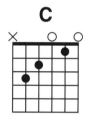

Mandolin

G	D	Em	C
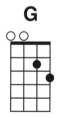	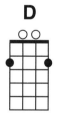		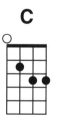

Banjo

G	D	Em	C
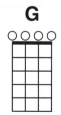		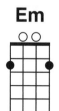	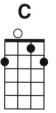

Wagon Wheel

Words and Music by Bob Dylan and Ketch Secor

Verse
Moderately fast

Chorus

Additional Lyrics

2. Runnin' from the cold up in New England,
   I was born to be a fiddler in an old-time string band.
   My baby plays the guitar; I pick a banjo now.
   Oh, north country winters keep a gettin' me down.
   Lost my money playin' poker, so I had to leave town.
   But I ain't turnin' back to livin' that old life no more.

3. Walkin' through the south out of Roanoke,
   I caught a trucker out of Philly, had a nice long toke.
   But he's a headed west from the Cumberland Gap
   To Johnson City, Tennessee.
   And I gotta get a move on before the sun.
   I hear my baby callin' my name and I know that
   She's the only one.
   And if I die in Raleigh, at least I will die free.

125

Standard Ukulele

D	G6	E	G
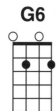	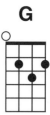	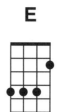	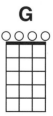

Baritone Ukulele

D	G6	E	G
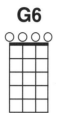	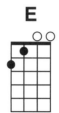		

Guitar

D	G6	E	G
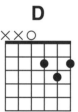	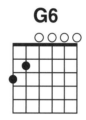	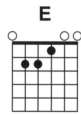	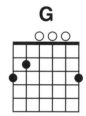

Mandolin

D	G6	E	G
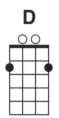	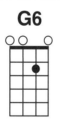		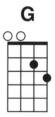

Banjo

D	G6	E	G
	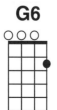		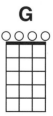

Walk on the Wild Side

Words and Music by Lou Reed

Verse
Moderately

1. Hol - ly came from Mi - am - i, F - L - A, hitch-hiked her way a-cross the U. S.
2. – 5. *See additional lyrics*

A. ___ Plucked her eye - brows on the way, shaved her legs _ and then he was a she. She says,

"Hey, babe, take a walk on the wild side." ___ Said, "Hey, hon - ey, take a walk on the

1., 3., 4.

wild side."

2., 5.

wild side." And the col-ored girls go:

Chorus

Do, do, do, do, do, do, ___ do, do, do, do, do, do, do, do, ___ do, do.

Do, do, do, do, do, do, ___ do, do, do, do, do, do, do, do, ___ do, do.

To Coda ⊕
D.C. al Coda
(take repeats) ⊕ **Coda**

Do.

Additional Lyrics

2. Candy came from out on the Island.
   In the back room she was everybody's darling.
   But she never lost her head, even when she was giving head.
   She says, "Hey, babe, take a walk on the wild side."
   Said, "Hey, babe, take a walk on the wild side."

3. Little Joe never once gave it away.
   Everybody had to pay and pay.
   A hustle here and a hustle there,
   New York City is the place where they said,
   "Hey, babe, take a walk on the wild side."
   I said, "Hey, Joe, take a walk on the wild side."

4. Sugar Plum Fairy came and hit the streets,
   Looking for soul food and a place to eat.
   Went to the Apollo; you should've seen 'em go, go, go.
   They said, "Hey, sugar, take a walk on the wild side."
   I said, "Hey, babe, take a walk on the wild side."

5. Jackie is just speeding away.
   Thought she was James Dean for a day.
   Then I guess she had to crash;
   Valium would have helped that bash.
   She said, "Hey, babe, take a walk on the wild side."
   I said, "Hey, honey, take a walk on the wild side."

Standard Ukulele

G	C	Em	D	Cm	Bm	A7	E♭7
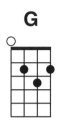	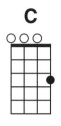					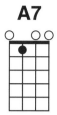	

Baritone Ukulele

G	C	Em	D	Cm	Bm	A7	E♭7
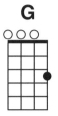		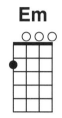	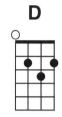				

Guitar

G	C	Em	D	Cm	Bm	A7	E♭7
	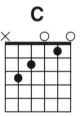	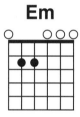	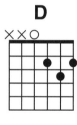	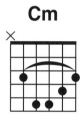	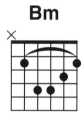	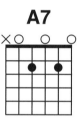	

Mandolin

G	C	Em	D	Cm	Bm	A7	E♭7 (5fr)
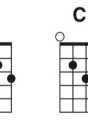	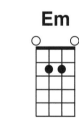			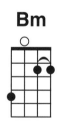			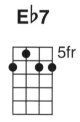

Banjo

G	C	Em	D	Cm	Bm	A7	E♭7
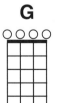	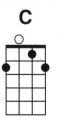	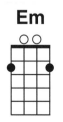			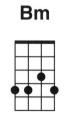	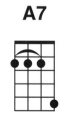	

The Way I Am
Words and Music by Ingrid Michaelson

Standard Ukulele

C 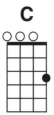 Em 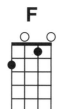 F 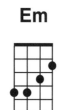 G

Baritone Ukulele

C 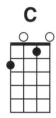 Em 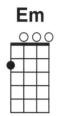 F  G

Guitar

C 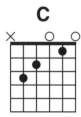 Em 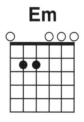 F  G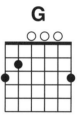

Mandolin

C 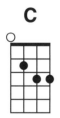 Em  F  G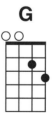

Banjo

C  Em 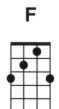 F 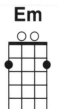 G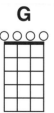

The Weight

By Jaime Robbie Robertson

Verse
Moderately slow

1. I pulled in - to Naz - a - reth, was feel - in' 'bout half - past dead.
2. – 5. *See additional lyrics*

I just need some - place ____ where I can lay ____ my head. ____

"Hey, mis - ter, can you tell me where a man might find a bed?" ____

He just grinned and shook my hand. ____ "No" was all ____ he said.

Chorus

Take a load off, Fan - ny. Take a load for free. ____

Take a load off, Fan - ny, and ____ you put the load right on me.

Additional Lyrics

2. I picked up my bag, I went looking for a place to hide
   When I saw Carmen and the devil walking side by side.
   I said, "Hey, Carmen, come on, let's go downtown."
   She said, "I gotta go, but my friend can stick around."

3. Go down, Miss Moses, there's nothing you can say.
   It's just ol' Luke and Luke's waiting on the judgment day.
   "Well, Luke, my friend, what about young Anna Lee?"
   He said, "Do me a favor, son.
   Won't you stay and keep Anna Lee company?"

4. Crazy Chester followed me and he caught me in the fog.
   He said, "I will fix your rack if you'll take Jack, my dog."
   I said, "Wait a minute, Chester, you know I'm a peaceful man."
   He said, "That's okay, boy. Won't you feed him when you can?"

5. Catch a Cannonball now, to take me down the line.
   My bag is sinking low and I do believe it's time
   To get back to Miss Fanny. You know she's the only one
   Who sent me here with her regards for everyone.

Standard Ukulele

Bm	Em	A	G	D

Baritone Ukulele

Bm	Em	A	G	D

Guitar

Bm	Em	A	G	D

Mandolin

Bm	Em	A	G	D
			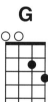	

Banjo

Bm	Em	A	G	D

Wellerman

New Zealand Folksong

Verse
Moderately fast

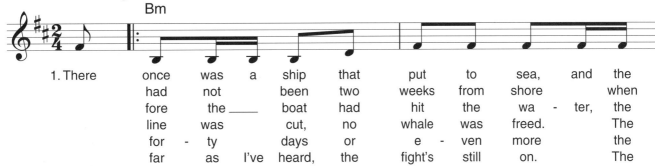

1. There once was a ship that put to sea, and the
had not been two weeks from shore when
fore the ____ boat had hit the wa - ter, the
line was cut, no whale was freed. The
for - ty days or e - ven more the
far as I've heard, the fight's still on. The

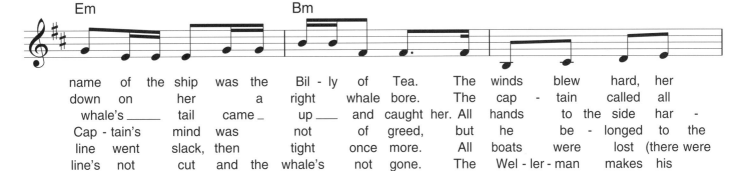

name of the ship was the Bil - ly of Tea. The winds blew hard, her
down on her a right whale bore. The cap - tain called all
whale's ____ tail came ____ up ____ and caught her. All hands to the side har -
Cap - tain's mind was not of greed, but he be - longed to the
line went slack, then tight once more. All boats were lost (there were
line's not cut and the whale's not gone. The Wel - ler - man makes his

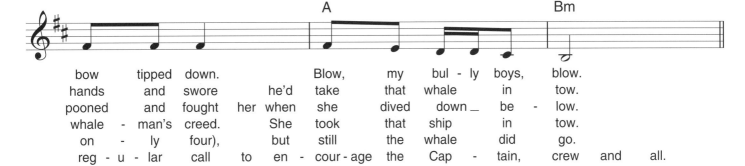

bow tipped down. Blow, my bul - ly boys, blow.
hands and swore he'd take that whale in tow.
pooned and fought her when she dived down ____ be - low.
whale - man's creed. She took that ship in tow.
on - ly four), but still the whale did go.
reg - u - lar call to en - cour - age the Cap - tain, crew and all.

Chorus

Soon may the Wel - ler - man come to bring us sug - ar and

tea and rum. One day when the ton - guin' is done, we'll

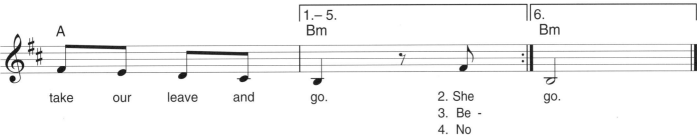

1. – 5.

6.

take our leave and go. go.

2. She
3. Be -
4. No
5. For
6. As

Standard Ukulele

D	G	Cmaj7	C	Em	Am
		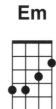			

Baritone Ukulele

D	G	Cmaj7	C	Em	Am

Guitar

D	G	Cmaj7	C	Em	Am

Mandolin

D	G	Cmaj7	C	Em	Am

Banjo

D	G	Cmaj7	C	Em	Am

Why Walk When You Can Fly

Words and Music by Mary Chapin Carpenter

Verse
Moderately, in 2

1. In this world there's a whole lot of trou-ble, ba-by. In this world there's a
2. In this world there's a whole lot of sor - row. __ In this world there's a
3. In this world there's a whole lot of gold - en. __ In this world there's a

whole lot of pain. In this world there's a whole lot of trou-ble but a
whole lot of shame. In this world there's a whole lot of sor - row and a
whole lot of plain. In this world you've a soul for a com-pass and a

whole lot of ground __ to gain. Why take when you could be
whole lot of ground __ to gain. When you spend your __ whole life
heart for a pair __ of wings. There's a star on the far ho -

Chorus

giv - ing? Why watch as the world __ goes by? It's a
wish - ing, want - ing and won-der - ing why, it's a
ri - zon ris - ing bright in an az - ure sky. For the

hard e-nough life to be liv - ing. Why ⎱
long e-nough life to be liv - ing. Why ⎰ walk when you __ can fly?
rest of the time that you're giv - en, why ⎰

Interlude

| D | G | Cmaj7 | C | D | G | Cmaj7 | C |

| D | G | Cmaj7 | C | Em | 1., 2. C | 3. C |

Standard Ukulele

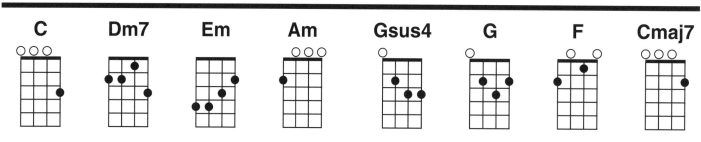

Baritone Ukulele

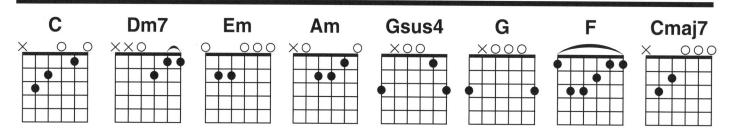

Guitar

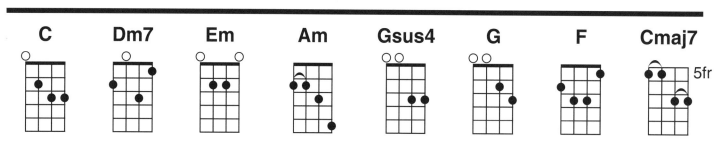

Mandolin

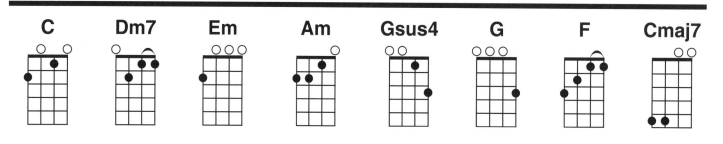

Banjo

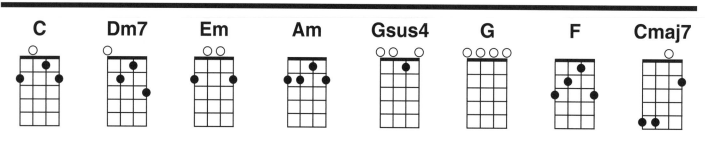

Woman
Words and Music by John Lennon

Verse
Moderately

1. Wom-an, I can hard-ly ex-press my mixed e-mo-tions at my
2. Wom-an, I know you un-der-stand the lit-tle child in-

thought-less-ness. After all, I'm for-ev-er in your debt. And
side the man. Please re-mem-ber, my life is in your hands. And

wom-an, I will try to ex-press my in-ner feel-ings and
wom-an, hold me close to your heart. How-ev-er dis-tant, don't
3. Wom-an, please let me ex-plain. I nev-er meant to cause you

thank-ful-ness for show-ing me the mean-ing of suc-
keep us a-part. After all, it is writ-ten in the
sor-row or pain. So let me tell you a-gain and a-gain and a-

Chorus

cess. Oo, well,
stars. Oo, well,
gain. I love you, yeah,

well. Do, do, do, do, do. Oo, well,
well. Do, do, do, do, do. Oo, well,
yeah, now and for-ev-er. I love you, yeah,

To Coda ⊕   1. G   2. **D.S. al Coda** G   ⊕ **Coda**

well. Do, do, do, do, do. do, do. ev-er.
well, Do, do, do,
yeah, now and for-

Standard Ukulele

| C | Csus4 | Am | F | E7 | G | D7 |

   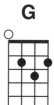 

Baritone Ukulele

| C | Csus4 | Am | F | E7 | G | D7 |

  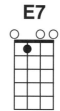 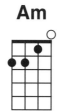 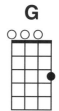 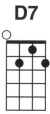

Guitar

| C | Csus4 | Am | F | E7 | G | D7 |

 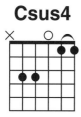 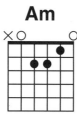  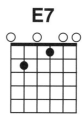 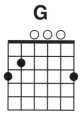 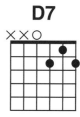

Mandolin

| C | Csus4 | Am | F | E7 | G | D7 |

      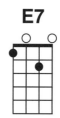 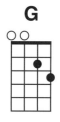 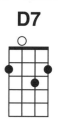

Banjo

| C | Csus4 | Am | F | E7 | G | D7 |

  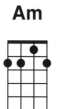   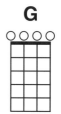 

You and I

Words and Music by Ingrid Michaelson

Standard Ukulele

Em	C	D	Bm	G	Am

Baritone Ukulele

Em	C	D	Bm	G	Am

Guitar

Em	C	D	Bm	G	Am
	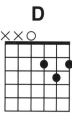		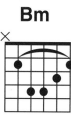		

Mandolin

Em	C	D	Bm	G	Am

Banjo

Em	C	D	Bm	G	Am

You're So Vain

Words and Music by Carly Simon

Verse
Moderately

Em / C

1. You walked in-to the par-ty like you were walk-ing on-to a yacht;
had me sev-er-al years a-go, when I was still quite na-ive.
hear you went up to Sar-a-to-ga, and your horse nat-'ral-ly won.

Em

your hat stra-te-gi-c'lly dipped be-low one eye, your
well, you said that we make such a pret-ty pair and
Then you flew your Lear jet up to No-va Sco-tia, to see the

C / Em / C D

scarf, it was ap-ri-cot. You had one eye in the mir-
that you would nev-er leave. But you gave a-way the things
to-tal e-clipse of the sun. Well, you're where you should be all

Bm Em / C / G / D

- ror as you watched your-self ga-votte, and all the girls
you loved and one of them was me. I had some dreams,
the time, and when you're not you're with some un-der-world spy

C

dreamed that they'd be your part-ner, they'd be your part-ner,
they were clouds in my cof-fee, clouds in my cof-fee, and
or the wife of a close friend, wife of a close friend,

Chorus

G / Am

you're so vain, you prob-'bly think this song is a-bout

G / Em / C

you. You're so vain, I'll bet you think this song is a-bout

D | 1., 2. | 3. | G

you. Don't you? Don't you? 2. Well, you you?
3. Well, I

Standard Ukulele

G   D   F   C   Dsus4   Dsus2

Baritone Ukulele

G   D   F   C   Dsus4   Dsus2

Guitar

G   D   F   C   Dsus4   Dsus2

Mandolin

G   D   F   C   Dsus4   Dsus2

Banjo

G   D   F   C   Dsus4   Dsus2

You've Got to Hide Your Love Away

Words and Music by John Lennon and Paul McCartney

Tuning

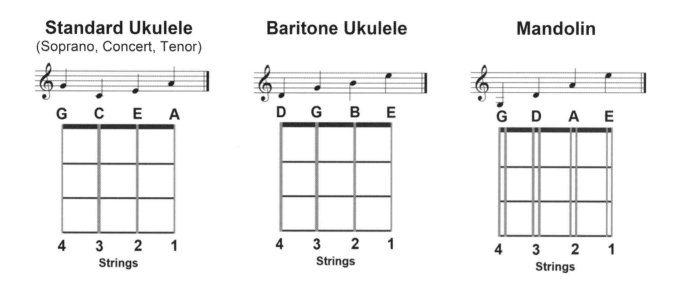

Standard Ukulele
(Soprano, Concert, Tenor)

G C E A

4 3 2 1
Strings

Baritone Ukulele

D G B E

4 3 2 1
Strings

Mandolin

G D A E

4 3 2 1
Strings

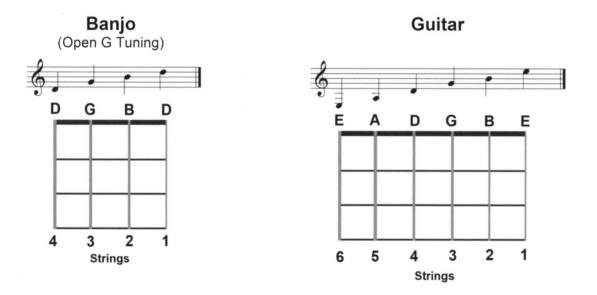

Banjo
(Open G Tuning)

D G B D

4 3 2 1
Strings

Guitar

E A D G B E

6 5 4 3 2 1
Strings

All banjo chord formations illustrated in this book are based on "Open G" tuning. If an alternate tuning is used the banjo player can read the chord letters for the songs and disregard the diagrams.